CIRCLE-TIME IN-SERVICE TRAINING MANUAL

Mollie Curry and Carolyn Bromfield

A NASEN Publication

Published by NASEN.
NASEN is a registered charity. Charity No. 1007023.
NASEN is a company limited by guarantee, registered in England and Wales.
Company No. 2674379.

Further copies of this book and details of NASEN's many other publications may be
obtained from the Publications Department at its registered office:
NASEN House, 4/5 Amber Business Village, Amber Close, Amington, Tamworth,
Staffs. B77 4RP.
Telephone: 01827 311500 Fax: 01827 313005
Email: welcome@nasen.org.uk

Cover Design by Graphic Images.
Typeset in Helvetica by J. C. Typesetting and printed in the United Kingdom by Stowes.

CIRCLE-TIME
In-service Training Manual

Contents

INTRODUCTION
Using the Manual

This manual provides six sessions of Circle-time training aimed at teachers of primary aged children. It is designed to be used by headteachers and other senior management, educational psychologists, academic councils, SENCOs, and other professionals who facilitate INSET for schools or groups of teachers. Each session is free-standing and can be used independently or used together they will provide a developmental progression for staff training.

The aim is to introduce Circle-time to those teachers new to the concept and to develop its use for those already conversant. Each session will encourage the adults in schools to focus and explore together in specific directions whilst highlighting the benefits to children of regular Circle-time work. The structure and organisation of Circle-time will vary but we have adhered to a set format to enable the facilitator to introduce all of the elements to the group (illustrated in OHP 2, page 60). Section 1 provides an introduction to Circle-time and describes in detail the various techniques used in the sessions. Each technique has been given a symbol for easy reference to enable the facilitator to refer to it at the appropriate juncture.

As advisory teachers working with children who have behaviour problems we have found Circle-time a useful tool in shaping desired behaviour (see page 10). Examining some of the common threads in our client group we found that nearly all the children exhibited signs of low self-esteem, poor social skills, limited friendship abilities and a difficulty in working in groups. Our training sessions are therefore based on topics that will enhance these skills. The first session is a general introduction to Circle-time and can be used with those teachers unfamiliar with the concept. This is followed by sessions on Feelings, Self-esteem, Friendship, Problem Solving and Dealing with Anger.

The contents of each session are designed for **adult** participation although some ideas could be transposed for classroom use. We therefore suggest that the facilitator makes the group aware of our other publication **Personal and Social Education Through Circle-time**, which will provide lesson plans for teachers to use with children. This book also provides a more detailed description of Circle-time and self-esteem and is therefore recommended as essential reading for all course leaders. The first session includes games from our original book because they are most suitable for illustrating how games can be used whereas the others are not duplicated but if there are favourites these can be repeated or different ones substituted.

As most training takes place after school or for half day periods we have designed 1 hour, 2 hour and 3 hour sessions.

Section 1 - Techniques

This section contains a short introduction plus all the essential elements of a comprehensive Circle-time programme. The techniques are described here in full to avoid constant repetition. The facilitator is therefore advised to refer to the relevant passage in this section each time the appropriate symbol is denoted in a training session.

CONTENTS:

Circle-time: A Description

Children with Behaviour Problems

Strategies for Managing Behaviour in the Circle

Games

Rules

Active Listening

The Round

The Activity

Conference

Special Person

Brainstorming

Questions and Answers

CIRCLE-TIME: A DESCRIPTION

Circle-time is a way of supporting children and enhancing self-esteem, of making a safe environment in which to take risks, to explore feelings, to discuss conflicts in a non-blaming, non-punitive way and a process that encourages children to believe that they are worthwhile people.

It is a time to foster a caring group feeling where each member is valued and valuable, where each child gets a chance to speak and more importantly a chance to be listened to. Circle-time is a time for children to discover more about themselves, their strengths, feelings, preferences, as well as discovering more about their peers. It is accomplished by affirming the positive attributes of self and others. It is a time when children find out more about themselves, what they are capable of and how they relate to one another.

There are lots of serious, lively discussions where feelings are discovered, explored and accepted. Children come to realise that if they understand themselves it will help them to understand others better. The value of co-operation and friendship is examined and emphasised using practical activities so that children (and the teacher) are involved in experiential learning.
Facilitator: Use OHP 1 on page 59.

The Aims of Circle-time

Circle-time is aimed at developing the unique potential of each individual, of looking at their social and emotional growth and nurturing this within a caring group environment. Circle-time provides the person-centred setting that allows for the development of communication systems built on respect for every person in which healthy positive relationships can flourish.

Children need to acquire the necessary social skills to enable them to live and work together in a harmonious atmosphere. Many children seem to acquire these skills naturally but some children come to school without them, which can lead to inappropriate interactions with the people they meet. This affects their work and can affect the academic progress of a whole class. Social skills can be taught to children and practised in the safety of Circle-time. Research demonstrates that learning is achieved most productively in groups where people can interact and reflect on mutual experiences.

Circle-time is also a structure for providing self-esteem enhancing activities. Many researchers have shown a positive correlation between children's self-esteem and their academic success (Coopersmith, 1981; Purkey, 1970; Burns, 1979; and Lawrence, 1987). Children who feel good about themselves learn more easily and retain information longer.

Self-esteem has been likened to having money

If you have money in your pocket then you can afford to take risks, try new things, because even if you lose a small amount there will still be some left. However, children with low self-esteem have little or no money and cannot afford to gamble as they run the risk of failing and being left with nothing.

Circle-time is a time for children to discover more about themselves, their strengths, feelings, preferences, as well as discovering more about others. This is done by affirming the positive attributes of self and others and offers mutual support to the whole group. Once children come to recognise their own emotions they are better placed to understand those of others. During this process isolated children are 'joined' in the group by the teacher acknowledging common feelings or thoughts. The group can begin to acquire the ability to look at things from another person's point of view and use this as a practice ground for recognising that other people have different perspectives. Pupils can begin to see quiet classmates in a new light which boosts the withdrawn child's self-esteem and through non-threatening activities, games and talking pairs, confidence can grow until the child feels able to participate fully with the whole class.

Circle-time is a vehicle for exploring personal and social issues. Children need to acquire the necessary social skills to enable them to work together, communicate effectively and form positive relationships. Friends play an important part in all our lives and the skills to build and maintain friendships can be taught in Circle-time. Problems such as playground conflicts, disruption in class and difficulties in relationships can be discussed in the safe environment of Circle-time. The possibility for finding solutions to these problems becomes achievable and as the children are part of this process their ownership and responsibility for the outcomes empowers them, leading to success. The group has a sense of counselling itself and all gain from finding solutions to problems that are causing unhappiness.

Circle-time is a time to foster a caring group feeling where each member is valued and made to feel valuable. Sitting in a circle creates an equal environment where everyone can be seen, where each child gets a chance to speak and more importantly a chance to be listened to, and everyone is special.

Circle-time enables children to participate as listeners and speakers and facilitates the whole process of communication.

The added benefit of Circle-time is that it covers many of the components of the English Attainment Targets in the *National Curriculum*. These include taking turns, knowing when to stop talking and wait for another's response, and listening attentively in a group situation.

English Key Stage 1

1. Range

a. Pupils should be given opportunities to talk for a range of purposes including:
❑ exploring, developing and clarifying ideas; predicting outcomes and discussing possibilities;
❑ describing events, observations and experiences; making simple, clear explanations of choices; giving reasons for opinions and actions.

2. Key Skills

a. Building on their previous experience, pupils should be encouraged to speak with confidence, making themselves clear through organising what they say and choosing words with precision. Pupils should be taught conventions of discussion and conversation e.g. taking turns in speaking.
b. Pupils should be encouraged to listen with growing attention and concentration.

English Key Stage 2

1. Range

a. Pupils should be given opportunities to talk for a range of purposes, including:
❑ exploring, developing and explaining ideas;
❑ sharing ideas, insights and opinions;
❑ reporting and describing events and observations.
b. Pupils should be given opportunities to listen and respond to a range of people. They should be taught to identify and comment on key features of what they see and hear in a variety of media.

2. Key Skills

a. Pupils should be encouraged to express themselves confidently and clearly. Pupils should be taught to evaluate their own talk and reflect on how it varies.
b. Pupils should be taught to listen carefully.
They should be encouraged to qualify or justify what they think after listening to other opinions or accounts and deal politely with opposing points of view.

Personal and Social Education development is central to the *National Curriculum* and all aspects of a school's P.S.E. curriculum can be addressed through Circle-time.

Children with Behaviour Problems

Children with behaviour difficulties need to be viewed in the context of the whole learning environment. Children's behaviour cannot be seen in isolation as behaviour is affected by the organisation and management of the classroom and by the social interaction of their peers and adults.

Children with behaviour problems have low self-esteem and are likely to act out all kinds of difficult behaviour based on a poor view of self. Both the level of self-esteem and the process through which self-esteem is determined are derived through relationships and interaction with others. The groups to which we belong and the social support they provide have important and powerful effects on our self-esteem. Group work such as Circle-time is an ideal forum for dealing with self-esteem and group members begin to account for their own behaviour as they begin to support one another through co-operative activities and games.

So many times children repeat the same ineffectual solution to a problem which leads to confrontation or rejection. Teachers are in a central position to develop and teach a wide range of strategies enabling children to have a real choice about their behaviour. Learning to deal with a conflict in a positive way enables those children who are socially skilled to become role models and a resource for others.

Through Circle-time children learn to ask for help from other children as well as the adults. Ideas can be practised in role-play situations that are non-blaming and non-judgmental. As each class builds up its own repertoire of solutions, individual repertoires widen and start to act as a preventative measure so that fewer conflicts arise in the class and in the playground. Together the class can work through its problems and work towards forming a cohesive group. The spirit of competition is replaced by an atmosphere of empathy and mutual assistance. Circle-time is effective in changing behaviour as it relies on group adherence - that sense of wanting to belong.

Interaction with group members provides support, gives opportunities and allows models for pro-social behaviour. The group will want to help the child with behaviour problems because there will be less discord in class, providing a better working atmosphere, and they will enjoy the opportunity to contribute to improving the situation. Behaviour is a set of skills and can be taught and learnt. These skills empower pupils to take increasing control and responsibility for their behaviour.

Strategies for Managing Behaviour in the Circle

1. It is important to plan a positive initiation to Circle-time. The first few sessions may need to be shorter with more games and lots of fun activities that will encourage children to want to participate and not disrupt. This way they will also look forward to the next session.

2. To begin with the groups' listening skills may not be very good so do not have long periods with only one person talking. Instead have lots of talking and listening in pairs where each person gets a chance to speak and listen with limited waiting.

3. Encourage appropriate pairings. Praise children who begin to take responsibility for wise choices of partner. Pair with a good role model. Use a 'buddy' system.

Circle-time
Sunshine Sticker
Awarded for Good Listening

4. Make your expectations of behaviour clear from the start. Devise Circle-time behaviour rules and refer to them. Reward children who are following the rules. Stickers and certificates work well.

5. Offer consequences as a choice. 'If you continue to disrupt the game you will have to leave the circle until the game is finished. The choice is yours.'

6. Ignore minor disruptions and instead give attention to the child or children behaving appropriately and specifically mention what they are being praised for. 'Well done Michael, I can see you are sitting quietly waiting for the magic microphone.' This avoids giving negative attention and states clearly the desired behaviour. As soon as you see the child behaving appropriately you must *catch them being good'* and praise them.

7. Games can be used as an incentive for completing an activity. 'When you have finished that work you can choose the concluding game.' Ask the child which games they prefer and involve them in some of the planning.

8. Give them a special job or responsibility.

9. If a child is finding Circle-time difficult it may be necessary to talk to them beforehand. Listen to any concerns and then together work out a plan of action for increased success. This may involve some form of a contract or chart. For example:
   Decide on a behaviour and reinforce with stickers on a chart every time the behaviour is observed. When the child has collected an agreed number of stickers then they receive a negotiated reward.

I will try not to call out in the 'round' during Circle-time.
Every time I manage this my teacher will give me a sticker.

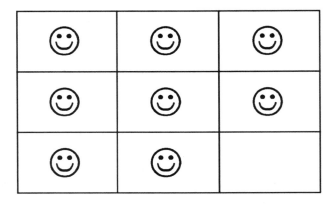

When I have collected 9 stickers the whole class can play parachute games.

This particular sticker chart encourages peer support for the child as everybody will participate in the reward.

Circle-Time Certificate

Awarded to _____

For _____

_____

_____

Signed _____ Date _____

An example of a certificate to reward desired behaviour.

GAMES

Games are included in Circle-time as they are not only fun activities with much affirming taking place when individuals are named or chosen, but they are also useful as starting points for further discussions. Games can be used as a warm-up activity for the group to get into the spirit of co-operation, working and playing together for fun. They can be used for concluding a session as a way of reuniting the group before going off to separate classroom activities and for enlivening the proceedings after a heavy discussion period. Games also allow for legitimate movement and are a good way to split inappropriate pairings or provide a solution to the gender divide where the girls sit on one side of the circle and the boys on the other!

Using Games

A game is an excellent teaching tool and can illustrate points for debate such as: 'Was there anyone not chosen?' 'How did it feel?' 'Could we as a group have done anything to avoid it happening?' These discussions could then be widened to encompass other areas of conflict such as the playground. The group could discuss how it might feel for children who do not have anyone to play with, or who do not get chosen for games, and the types of strategies they could employ to create a more harmonious, caring atmosphere. Very often this will lead children to establish rules or an agreed sign such as arms folded, legs crossed etc. to make sure everyone is included and to incorporate the notion of fair play.

Circle-time games are co-operative not competitive and winning is not an important factor.

Games are useful as they can:

1. provide a structure for learning;

2. defuse tension;

3. initiate group work skills;

4. build trust and sensitivity;

5. provide an opportunity for everyone to participate;

6. break down pupil/teacher barriers;

7. promote good communication;

8. improve group functioning;

9. increase self-awareness;

10. increase concentration and time on task;

11. improve listening skills;

12. encourage creativity and lateral thinking;

13. enhance academic achievement;

14. enhance self-esteem.

Games can be used as 'energy raisers'. After a game, great energy and enthusiasm can be put into work which follows, making games a great investment in time.

An important feature not to be ignored is Circle-time's potential for engendering fun and laughter. This is a primary motivation factor which ensures that pupils are always cued in to the 'here and now' and remain alert. If humour can be shared with pupils as a result of teachers participating as an equal member of the group, then it can function to strengthen relationships and create a more trusting climate.

Name Games

At the beginning of a new year or when somebody new enters a class, name games are important as they establish everyone's identity and help to bond the group. Using people's names is also a way of affirming each pupil in the class, of showing that they are a unique individual and someone who is special. They can be a 'spoonful of attention' for those who need it!

Mixing Games

It is beneficial for pupils to experience working with all the members of their group. This enables them to examine their thoughts, feelings and ideas and have dialogues with people who might have a different point of view or perspective to their own. It is easy and comfortable to always sit next to the same person or group of friends but mixing the pupils can encourage them to see others in a new light and be more tolerant of differences. Mixing games are a fun way to integrate the class, encourage the gender mix and anticipate behaviour problems before they arise.

RULES

Circle-time is flexible but, as with all successful structures, there needs to be some consensus of what is acceptable behaviour. Rules are important as they provide a framework within which relationships can develop and grow in a positive way. As with general classroom rules, it is best to have as few as possible, but to constantly reinforce and reward adherence. They need to be written up and displayed in the classroom and they need to be flexible to accommodate the changing needs of the group.

With young children three rules are sufficient and these could be:

1. Only one person speaks at a time.

2. We listen to the person who is speaking.

3. Have fun and make sure you don't spoil anybody else's fun!

Older children will be able to discuss the whole area of rules, perhaps starting with the rules they experience when playing games, what they thought their function was or if they thought they were fair. Pupils can brainstorm ideas for Circle-time rules, negotiate priorities with their peers and then select the ones they wish to operate. This way they will own the rules and therefore be much more likely to adhere to them. They constitute a **contract** between group members and include the important issue of **confidentiality**. Eventually members will begin to take responsibility for their behaviour and remind one another when they transgress. This takes the pressure away from the teacher being the law-enforcing authority, as children learn from one another, rather than being dictated to.

Some examples of rules which groups have evolved:

- Listen to one another.
- Talk one at a time.
- Respect the ideas and values of others.
- Anything said in the circle is confidential.
- The right to pass is always there.
- It's OK to make mistakes, as they are valuable learning points.
- Keep agreements that are made with the group.
- Do not hurt anybody either physically or verbally.

ACTIVE LISTENING

An important aspect of any Circle-time activity is the skill of **active listening**. This is a skill that both children and adults need to practise. We often think we are listening, but giving our full attention when someone is speaking is a skill we all need to cultivate.

Facilitator: Use OHP 3 on page 61.

Active listening can be defined as:

1. having eye contact with the person who is talking;

2. giving full attention;

3. sitting quietly without distracting the person who is speaking;

4. focusing on the speaker's needs;

5. showing that you understand;

6. letting the speaker express feelings without interruptions or 'put-downs';

7. asking no questions;

8. making no comments of your own;

9. showing you are listening by smiling, nodding etc. at appropriate times;

10. communicating acceptance - that no matter what is said the speaker is still OK.

Active listening is important to provide an atmosphere of co-operation and mutual regard. This is also beneficial to teachers as they no longer need to be agreeing, disagreeing, arguing, praising or blaming and can therefore take a neutral role which enables others in the group to express their feelings. Listening skills represent a necessary step in the effective functioning of Circle-time.

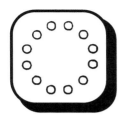

THE ROUND

Discussion time usually takes the form of a **round**. The round is an opportunity for each person in the circle to make a statement or a contribution to whatever the group is discussing. One person starts, sometimes with an opening tag line and the turn moves round the circle until everyone who wants to has had the opportunity to contribute. No one may comment on what anyone else has said and this includes the teacher.

One person speaking at a time, and everyone else listening, is an important Circle-time rule. It gives everyone an equal chance to contribute without being shouted down or ridiculed. It also encourages the quieter children to participate and denies the more vocal elements of the class the chance to dominate.

To facilitate the rule of only one person talking at a time, especially with younger children, it is sometimes useful to have a tangible object to pass round indicating whose turn it is to speak and this is often known as the **magic microphone**. An alternative to this is a **talk ticket** which is a piece of card that again is a visible signal to remind everyone that only the person with the ticket can talk.

The aim of a round is to provide a structure to get children to communicate with one another. All ideas are valued equally. The opportunity to *'pass'* is there for each individual as this is not to be a threatening time where pupils believe they are going to be forced to do something against their will. This would be totally counter-productive to the aims of Circle-time. Initially no comment should be made about pupils who pass because if rounds are introduced in a very non-threatening way then children can begin to enjoy the experience and see that there are no right or wrong answers and that whatever is said is OK. If pupils pass just say something like: 'It's all right! I expect you need some thinking time. We'll come back to you.' At the end of the round ask again. Very often, a response is then offered as ideas are shared and thoughts triggered.

For young children rounds can start off with simple tag lines such as:

'My favourite colour is...'
'My best friend is...'
'My favourite TV programme is...'
'I feel happy when...'
'I feel sad when...'

Later, as the pupils become accustomed to this way of working, they can choose topics to discuss which arise from incidents in school or in the playground, and then use them as a forum for brainstorming ideas and strategies as a means of resolving conflicts.

This gives the chance to explore self-awareness in a positive way before leading on to more sensitive areas. It takes time to build trust where children feel comfortable exploring personal feelings with other group members. It also takes a while for children to recognise the importance of establishing trust, for them to trust another person, to have a valid comment and for them to exhibit that trust by respecting their words without interruption or comment.

Problems can occur with this technique when children are first starting or when there are large numbers in a class. It may be unreasonable to ask children to sit for a long period of time without an activity other than 'active listening' as they can become distracted which in turn could lead to them disturbing others. If these problems are occurring, use the whole class round less frequently. Instead ask children to share ideas in pairs, threes or fours. This way everybody is occupied and it also encourages shy children to participate as they are only having to face an audience of one, two or three. Feedback can be given by appointing a spokesperson from each group.

Double Circles

A variation on the round is double circles. The inner circle faces outwards and the outer circle faces in. Each person sits opposite a partner. A subject or tag line is given for discussion and taking it in turns each pupil talks and then listens. Initially pupils may need to be labelled A and B so that first of all the A's talk and the B's listen, and then they swap. After an appropriate time, a signal is given and the inner circle move one space to the right. The same subject can be used or a new development introduced. Each time the circle moves everyone has a new partner and can hear new ideas or rehearse thoughts and opinions.

It is then possible to return to a large circle to report back to the group on your partner's interests or thoughts on a subject, providing you have their permission. This introduces another element as concentration and good listening skills are necessary for effective and accurate reporting to take place.

THE ACTIVITY

The activity is the central part of any Circle-time around which the other components hinge. It is therefore essential that this section is well prepared so that children are not kept waiting whilst the teacher organises resources. Inappropriate behaviour can very quickly develop if children have nothing to do or if they think the teacher's attention is engaged elsewhere.

Teachers need to be aware that the pairings or grouping of children may need to be managed in order to ensure that children are given the opportunity to work with many different people and to feel comfortable about doing so. Care also needs to be taken to make sure that certain children do not become isolated or continually rejected.

CONFERENCE

The conference section of Circle-time is a crucial element. It follows each activity and allows for discussion and evaluation of the subject. It is a time to encourage children to offer their ideas, thoughts, feelings and for the teacher to also have an input in order to steer the discussion in certain directions if necessary, so that children understand the point of the exercise. The conferencing needs to be carefully thought out in order to stimulate appropriate responses with questions such as:

How will that work?

How will that affect other people?

How do people feel about that?

Children also need to be reminded of the confidentiality rule - that we do not name individuals when talking about anything negative. Children can say something like, 'I felt very upset yesterday when someone teased me and called me a name.'

The conference section will also allow teachers to evaluate the success of each Circle-time as they receive feedback from the group which will be helpful in any future planning.

SPECIAL PERSON

During Circle-time one of the children's favourite times is choosing a special person for the day. This is an opportunity for the group to affirm an individual by asking everyone in the circle to say something positive about the pupil. The person chosen usually waits outside the room to heighten anticipation and keep the surprise total. Young children are invited to go outside with a friend and share a book. While the chosen child is outside each person affirms the special person and the affirmations are recorded in some way so that they will be a tangible memento for the pupil to keep.

Older children can record their own statements on a piece of paper which can be collected to form a booklet or the teacher can scribe the comments on a large sheet of paper in the centre of the circle. This is usually done in the form of a 'round' to enable pupils to listen to one another's comments and even if the comments at first seem a little superficial, practice and good role-modelling from the teacher and peers will encourage pupils to look beneath the surface and discover the positive attributes in every child. It is helpful to start the process by using the most popular children as the class will have no difficulty in finding positive attributes. Once the class becomes skilled and sensitive, other children can be included until everybody has had a turn. Other ideas are special person certificates or posters. Finding the meaning of a child's name can add a fresh dimension and enhance their reputation.

When the list is complete, the special person is invited back into the centre of the circle or by the teacher's side, and the list is read out to them. To witness the response of children who take part in this special day and see them 'beam from ear to ear' as their list is read is almost justification alone for continuing Circle-time. This gives a tremendous boost to self-esteem.

The special person may be awarded a certificate or given a special badge denoting the event. They may be allowed to pick a name for themselves for the day or be allowed some special privileges such as choosing a game, being first in the line, having extra time on the computer etc. The children enjoy these privileges and the rest of the class see them as being fair as everybody will get a turn at being special and they are rewarded for just being themselves.

BRAINSTORMING

Note to facilitator: This technique does not have a symbol but is a very effective method of gathering information and should be explained to teachers.

The four main purposes of brainstorming are:

1. To produce a large number of ideas quickly.

2. To encourage pupils to think creatively and look for original ideas.

3. To involve the whole class and show that we value everybody's ideas.

4. To show that by working co-operatively we can achieve more than the individual can alone.

Ideas can be written down on a central piece of paper and the teacher can act as a scribe for younger children. The atmosphere should be non-judgmental with everybody's ideas being valued and written down - no matter how impractical - without being commented on. The teacher, who is also part of the group, can add ideas, scattering them in a random order so as not to perceive one as being better than another.

When the flow of ideas ceases it is a good idea to wait for a few minutes so that children can understand that they are responsible for their own learning and that the teacher is not there dictating terms. Silence gives an opportunity for reflective thinking and it takes the teacher away from 'rescue' mode. It often seems second nature for teachers to leap in and rescue the situation whenever there is an awkward silence. This handing over of responsibility of learning to our pupils is something that we as teachers need to cultivate.

After the pupils have exhausted their suggestions the list should be reviewed. Categorise and simplify if appropriate or list the ideas in some order of importance. The group is then in a better position to make choices and decisions.

This is a useful tool when discussing **behaviour** as pupils are stimulated into donating ideas to solve problems which can lead to the formation of a bank of solutions for pupils to try in similar circumstances. This will ultimately help to provide positive role models for unskilled children and arm them with a list of strategies to attempt.

The fact that all contributions are accepted and anonymous, that no one is excluded or evaluated, that most of the time they are not under the watchful eye of the teacher (busy acting as a scribe) all add up to a positive feeling within the group.

Questions and Answers

The following section contains a set of questions and answers commonly asked at INSET sessions.

Q. Why is the shape important?

A. Sitting in a circle is important as it ensures that everyone (even the teacher) is equal; everyone can be seen and heard; people can make eye contact which is an important aspect of speaking and listening; there are no physical barriers such as desks and chairs and everyone is valued as an important member of the group. Sitting in a circle also reduces distracting behaviours such as chatting and fiddling as everyone in the circle can be seen.

Q. There isn't enough room in my class for a circle. What can I do?

A. In our experience there aren't many rooms that can't be transformed with a little bit of foresight and planning. If the furniture has to be rearranged to accommodate Circle-time then it is helpful to plan your session for after playtime in the morning or first thing in the afternoon. This allows you and some children from your class time to stack the desks or tables and get the room ready. We have found that even reception class children can become very adept at furniture removals! At the end of a session the furniture can be quickly put back by the whole class if they are given clear and concise instructions.

In those classrooms where it is impossible to move the furniture or the shape is too constricting to form a circle we recommend timetabling a hall period or using a bigger room such as the library.

Q. How often should I have Circle-time? How long should it be?

A. The frequency and duration of Circle-time is governed by varying levels of concentration and the constraints of the curriculum. Some teachers have found they prefer to have shorter sessions more than once a week whilst others have opted for at least an hour a week of good quality Circle-time. Remember that younger children need more active participation as they cannot sit and listen for long periods and that older children can plan and lead their own circles. This is the advantage of Circle-time - the fact that it is flexible and can be designed to meet the needs of you and your class.

Q. My class sit in a circle to tell me their news on a Monday. Am I doing Circle-time?

A. Sitting in a circle can be beneficial for all sorts of lessons and some teachers even call the registers with the children sitting in a circle but this is NOT Circle-time.

Q. What's the point of the games?

A. Games are used as a warm-up exercise to enliven the group and get them into the spirit of co-operation, ready for the central activity. Games allow for legitimate movement and are a good way to split inappropriate pairings or get rid of the gender divide where the girls are on one side of the circle and the boys are on the other. Children like the fun element of Circle-time and they can be used as an inducement for completing an activity task. Games are also a very useful teaching tool as they can initiate discussion or be used to illustrate a point.

Q. What if a child does not want to speak in the round?

A. The right to 'pass' should always be there but when children are first introduced to Circle-time we find it helpful to make rounds non-threatening and tag lines easy to answer. This encourages children to participate. The teacher could say something like: 'I can see you need some more thinking time. We'll come back to you.' Children can be told that it's all right to use the same ending as someone else in the circle if they are finding it difficult. Children who don't speak at first are often listening to what is going on and participate by passing the 'magic microphone'. Later as their confidence grows they will begin to join in.

Q. There are one or two children who speak for a long time and 'take over' the circle. What can I do?

A. Be very precise about your instructions and start by saying that you only want one word answers to the tag lines. Thank the children when they have done this and explain that everyone in the circle is equal and that if some children have a lot to say they could be encouraged to put their ideas in a think book or journal.

Section 2 - Circle-time Sessions

This section contains the actual in-service session plans required by a facilitator to enable them to run Circle-time courses for teachers. The sessions can be used independently or as part of a developmental programme for a school or group.

CONTENTS:

CIRCLE-TIME INSET
Session 1 - Introduction to Circle-time
Time: 1 hour

Facilitator: We usually start Circle-time by greeting one another and this can be done in a number of ways:

 **GAMES**

NAME GAME - Name Clap
Everyone claps a rhythm together and then says the name of each person one at a time, going around the circle. For example: Clap knees (twice), clap hands (twice), then say the first person's name. 'Knees, hands, Mollie. Knees, hands, Carolyn. Knees, hands...' Continue round the circle until everyone has had a turn at being affirmed.

Facilitator: Each person has the spotlight for a few seconds and this is a *'spoonful of attention'* for everyone.

When starting Circle-time we allow the children to sit where they like as this provides a relaxed atmosphere. However, it is possible to move children around by using mixing games which enables the teacher to break up unlikely pairings and encourage a mix of genders. It also allows children to work with different members of the class and talk to children with whom they would not normally make contact.

Mixing games are a fun way to integrate the class:

MIXING GAME -There's a Space On My Right
Sit in a circle with one extra empty space. The person who has the empty chair on their right says: 'There's a space on my right and I would like ... to sit in it.' The chosen person moves to the space leaving their chair empty. The game proceeds in the same way.

USING GAMES
Facilitator: When you play this game with your class you may find that some children will not get chosen or the game will stop because two people keep choosing each other. This gives an opportunity to look at how it feels not to be chosen or about being left out.

Brainstorm the feelings and talk about the need for a rule to make it fair. Children are very quick to realise that we need to include everyone in the circle and that an agreed signal such as folding your arms once you have been chosen can be helpful. As with everything else this needs to be negotiated with your class so that it is personal to them and there is ownership of the problem and its solution. This discussion can then be related to events that might occur in the playground and illustrates how games can be used to learn new skills or help solve problems.

RULES

Facilitator: This is also the time to introduce a few simple rules:

1. Only one person talks at a time. Everyone else listens.

2. Show that you are listening by looking at the person who is speaking.

3. Everyone is included and has a turn.

4. Everyone has the right to have fun.
   No one can spoil anyone else's fun.

ACTIVE LISTENING

Facilitator: An important aspect of any Circle-time activity is the skill of 'active listening'.

This is a skill that both children and adults need to work at to develop. Active listening means:

1. Focusing on the speaker's needs.

2. Being there for the other person.

3. Showing you understand.

4. Letting the speaker express their feelings without interruptions or 'put-downs'.

5. Common acceptance - that no matter what is said the speaker is still OK.

THE ROUND

Facilitator: The group will get a chance to practise their active listening in the next section which is the round.

The round is an opportunity for each person to make a statement or contribution to whatever the group is discussing.

This is an opportunity for the teacher to 'join' together children who have similar ideas and for them to gain an insight into one another and recognise the ways in which they are alike and in which they differ.

Note to facilitator: It is helpful at this point to explain what the first tag line is and give an example, then ask for someone in the circle to start the round.

'The world would be a better place if people would ...'

THE ACTIVITY

Facilitator: When teachers have large classes it is advisable not to have a round too often as children with concentration problems will have too long to wait before actively participating. However, it is extremely important to practise listening skills and teachers need to devise different ways of getting children to speak and listen. A variation on the round is double circles. The inner and outer circle face towards each other and each person sits opposite a partner. If the numbers are even then the teacher observes and if the numbers are odd then the teacher joins in. A subject or tag line is given for discussion with each person taking it in turns to speak whilst the other listens. Teachers may need to number the pairs and tell the A's to speak first and remind the children about their active listening skills. The inner circle then moves one space to the right to face a new partner. The topic for discussion could be exactly the same and in some cases is very helpful, especially to children who find public speaking difficult as this gives them the opportunity to practise their answers with different partners and so gain confidence. This is an example of double circles.

Facilitator: The topic for discussion is 'groups'.

1. Ask the first pairing to tell each other about a group they have belonged to e.g. school, church, sport etc. When both partners have had a chance to speak and an opportunity to be listened to then the inner circle moves one space to the right so that everybody has a different partner.

2. The new pair tell each other what their feelings were when they first joined any of these groups. After each pair has finished the inner circle again moves one space to the right.

3. Ask the final pair to discuss strategies they used to help them cope with joining the group.

 # CONFERENCE

Facilitator: Re-form the large circle. Take three sheets of paper with the headings:

GROUPS   FEELINGS   STRATEGIES

Ask the members of the circle to record on the relevant sheets the information and ideas they discussed with their partners.

This activity illustrates a method for exploring all sorts of problems where children can discuss feelings, share ideas, and brainstorm solutions that will add to what they already know and give them new ideas to try out and evaluate. For example, children could discuss the issue of teasing and examine various coping strategies which could be recorded in a class book and evaluated at a later date.

 # SPECIAL PERSON

One of the children's favourite parts of Circle-time is choosing a special person for the day. This is an opportunity for the group to affirm an individual by asking everyone in the group to say something positive about the chosen person. The affirmations are then written down by the teacher whilst the special person waits outside the room. They are then invited back for the list to be read out which is then given to them to take home.

Note to facilitator: Enlarge special person list below and use as an example.

> **The special person today is**
> Liam
> **His name means**
> determined protector
> **He is special because:**
>
> He's co-operative and does not mind who he works with.
> He's generous, caring and kind.
> He hums when he's happy and we like that.
> He thinks of others and is aware of their needs.
> He concentrates.
> He has a good attitude to work.
> He's 'radical' in the playground and we enjoy his fun!

 **GAMES**

CONCLUDING GAME - Rain Forest

The whole group works together to form the sound of a tropical rain storm. The leader starts by rubbing their hands together. This is copied by the person to their left and so on around the circle until it reaches the leader and everyone is rubbing their hands together. The leader then changes the action to increase the sound as the storm builds up. Actions:

1. Rub hands.

2. Snap fingers.

3. Slap legs.

4. Stamp feet.

As with any sudden shower, the volume decreases and this is done by reversing the actions until everyone holds out the palms of their hands to face the circle in silence as the rain ends and peace descends.

Remember to copy the actions of the person next to you and not the leader!

CIRCLE-TIME INSET
Session 2 - Focus on Feelings
Time: 1 hour

Facilitator: Being able to identify and recognise feelings is an essential ingredient to a successful Circle-time. Through discussions and activities children can explore and share feelings which enables them to understand themselves better and leads to a greater understanding of other people's feelings and emotions.

Children who learn to express feelings realise they are not alone; that others have the same fears and anxieties.

The skills that are practised empower children by broadening their range of responses. In sharing and discussing feelings the opportunity presents itself to talk through and see problems in a different light.

Children need to learn to express their feelings in a variety of ways and different mediums can be used to explore these emotions. One way is to use games.

 **GAMES**

WARM UP GAME - Ping Pong

One person starts by saying 'Ping' and turns their head to the right or left. The person who receives the 'Ping' passes it on to the next person and so on round the circle. The 'Ping' can be made to go in the opposite direction by saying 'Pong'. It can then go back and forth like a game of ping pong.

Facilitator: When children first play this game they will all want to keep changing direction which means that a large number of pupils will be excluded. This provides an excellent opportunity to stop and talk about what they think is happening and about the *feelings* engendered. Brainstorm the *feelings* and discuss strategies for solving the problem. Often children will realise the need for a rule in this game such as 'You are only allowed to say "pong" once' and through practice will begin to co-operate with one another so that if they see people being excluded they will not change direction even if they have not used their turn. Children can become very skilled at being responsible for keeping the game flowing and involving everyone.

Recording Feelings

Feelings can be elicited from children and written on paper to be displayed on a 'feelings board'. These may then be transferred to a book which can be compiled as a reference to extend children's vocabulary.

RULES

Facilitator: This is also the time to introduce a few simple rules.

1. Only one person talks at a time. Everyone else listens.

2. Show that you are listening by looking at the person who is speaking.

3. Everyone is included and has a turn.

4. Everyone has the right to have fun. No one can spoil anyone else's fun.

ACTIVE LISTENING

1. Focusing on the speaker's needs.

2. Being there for the other person.

3. Showing you understand.

4. Letting the speaker express their feelings without interruptions or 'put downs'.

5. Common acceptance - that no matter what is said the speaker is still OK.

Facilitator: Active listening is important as it provides an atmosphere of co-operation and mutual regard which will enable children to freely express their feelings.

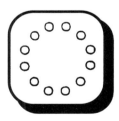

THE ROUND

This is a chance to practise active listening. Rounds can be started with tag lines such as:

'I feel happy when...'
'I feel sad when...'

'I feel proud when...'
'When I'm not chosen I feel...'
'When I have to read I feel...'

This is an opportunity for the teacher to 'join together' children who have similar feelings.

THE ACTIVITY

Feeling Excluded or Exclusive

Facilitator: You will need a sheet of coloured adhesive dots (four or five different colours depending on the size of the group).

Walk round the circle and put a coloured dot on everyone's back so that they cannot see what colour they are. Make some of the groups different sizes and at least one with only two or three people in it.
When they each have a dot give the instruction that they are to get into coloured groups *without talking!*

CONFERENCE

Each *group* discusses what their feelings were when they were involved in the activity.

❏ What did it feel like to be in a small group?

❏ What did it feel like to be in a big group?

❏ What strategies did they use to get into groups?

❏ If they were in a big group did they feel superior to those in a small group?

Re-form the large circle
❏ Share the different group feelings engendered by this activity.

❏ How can this be related to experiences children have in school?

❑ What lessons can be learnt?

Facilitator: Even though this activity is designed for use with adults be aware of those you select to go in the very small group. We all have feelings!

Feelings and the Curriculum

For work on feelings started through Circle-time to be really effective the teacher needs to relate the whole curriculum to the topic and highlight, where appropriate, how emotions are affected by daily occurrences and behaviours.

❑ When teachers model feelings and share their feelings by telling pupils how they feel, it demonstrates that all of us share the experience of all emotions.

❑ Use 'I statements' to express disapproval of negative behaviour. 'When you … I feel…'

❑ Use drama and role play to explore feelings, reactions and their effects.

❑ Use clay etc. to model emotions.

❑ Draw or paint feelings. Use guided fantasy to visualise emotions.

❑ Evaluate lessons. Encourage children to say how they feel about different subjects.

❑ Use books and stories to illustrate emotions.

 **GAMES**

CONCLUDING GAME - The Rule of the Game

One person has to leave the room. The rest of the group think of a gesture or mannerism which will be the 'rule' of the game. The chosen person comes back into the circle and asks each person a question until they have guessed the 'rule'. For example: each person might fold their arms before answering the question or each person might cough after answering.

This is a very good game for highlighting verbal and non-verbal behaviour and how we can assess people's emotions and feelings by looking at their body language.

CIRCLE-TIME INSET
Session 3 - Focus on Self-esteem
Time: 1 hour

Facilitator: Teaching people to affirm one another is a fundamental process in Circle-time and will boost self-esteem. Using people's names is a powerful aspect of this process as it highlights people as individuals who are worthwhile in their own right.

 **GAMES**

NAME GAME - The Eating Alphabet
One person starts by introducing themselves and adding something they like eating beginning with the same letter of the alphabet as their name e.g 'I'm Carolyn and I like cakes' or 'I'm Alex and I like apples.'

Facilitator: This also gives the teacher the opportunity to 'join together' those children who like similar things.

GETTING TO KNOW PEOPLE - True or False
Turn to the person next to you. One person starts by introducing herself/himself by name and then gives three 'facts' about herself/himself - two are true and one must be false. An example might be:
'My birthday is in January, I have a pet dog and my favourite food is lobster.'
The other person has to guess which is the false statement.
The roles are then reversed and the exercise repeated.

USING GAMES
Note to Facilitator: It is important to have a discussion with the participants at the end of each games session and explain clearly what the purpose of the game was and to find out whether that matched with their experience.

❏ What was the purpose of this game?

❏ Was it to find out at least some true things about your partner?

❏ Was it to look at body language and non-verbal signals?

❏ How did it feel if you guessed correctly?

❏ Did it help you get to know someone?

RULES

Facilitator: This is the time to introduce a few simple rules.

1. Only one person talks at a time. Everyone else listens. The use of the 'magic microphone' or 'talk ticket' will help.

2. Show that you are listening by looking at the person who is speaking.

3. Everyone is included and has a turn.

4. Everyone has the right to have fun. No one can spoil anyone else's fun.

ACTIVE LISTENING

Facilitator: An important aspect of any Circle-time is the skill of 'active listening'. This is a skill that both children and adults need to work at to develop. Active listening means:

1. Focusing on the speaker's needs.

2. Being there for the other person.

3. Showing you understand.

4. Letting the speaker express their feelings without interruptions or 'put-downs'.

5. Common acceptance - that no matter what is said the speaker is still OK.

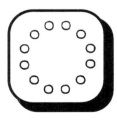

THE ROUND

'I feel really pleased when I ...'
'I am good at ...'

THE ACTIVITY

Facilitator: Write positive attributes on cards and display in the middle of the circle. Attributes such as the ability to be:

persistent	generous	happy
sincere	wise	understanding
reliable	calm	patient
talented	kind	efficient
quiet	responsible	cheerful
likeable	brave	interesting
energetic	clever	quick
trusty	friendly	sensible

Ask each person to choose three attributes they think describe themselves and write them down.

Work in pairs and tell each other why you have chosen those qualities and give examples.

Facilitator: This an opportunity to remind the group of their active listening skills.

Ask each person to select one attribute and give it to the person they have been talking to who returns it to them saying their name and the attribute e.g. 'Mollie, you are really brave.'

The partner answers: 'Thank you.'

Facilitator: Discuss the way we often try to reject compliments or minimise them e.g. 'Oh this old dress. I bought it in the sale.' As teachers we need to role model how to give and receive positive comments and Circle-time can provide lots of opportunities for children to practise this social skill.

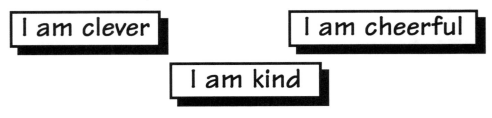

CONFERENCE

❑ Did you find this activity easy or was it hard?

❑ What was easy and what was difficult?

❑ Did you discover something about yourself you didn't know before?

❑ Can you say what that is?

❑ Did you find out something new about your partner? Discuss.

SPECIAL PERSON

Facilitator: This activity allows every participant (including the facilitator) to experience being 'special person'.

Paperbacks

Give each person a blank card (about 12cm x 20cm) on a piece of string or ribbon to go round their necks hanging down like a necklace. Then ask each person to turn their card to hang down their back.

Everyone is invited to write a positive comment on each person's card.

When this has been done the card can be turned round and read.

Watch the smiles!

GAMES

CONCLUDING GAME - Birthday Run

The facilitator calls out the months of the year and if your birthday is in that month you get up and find another chair.

The game can be repeated by calling out numbers from 1 to 31 and people have to find a different seat when the date of their birthday is called.

This game needs to be played quite quickly to keep the momentum going.

CIRCLE-TIME INSET
Session 4 - Focus on Friendship
Time: 1 hour

Facilitator: The ability to communicate effectively with others is a large part of being able to function interpersonally and an important task of childhood learning is to form positive relationships. Children need to understand how friendships are developed and maintained and in order for this to happen they must also acquire the ability to look at things from another person's point of view.

Friendships play an important part in every child's life and each new relationship enlarges a child's outlook on the world. Learning about others also affords the opportunity to learn more about themselves. Through the feedback that we receive from interactions with others we form a picture of ourselves. The more positive the interaction the more positive the view.

Friendships can be encouraged by Circle-time activities which have support built into the process.

 **GAMES**

WARM UP GAME - Six Things
The players pass an object round the circle. When the facilitator shouts 'Stop!', whoever has the object keeps it in their hands. The facilitator chooses a letter of the alphabet. The player with the object must immediately begin passing it round the circle again. They start by calling out one thing beginning with the chosen letter. The person next to them says another until six things (more if it is a large circle) have been called before the object gets back to the first person. The game is repeated starting from a different place.

Note to Facilitator: The letters X or Z should not be used. Make sure as many people as possible are involved in the game. Encourage players to help one another if their minds go blank! It is supposed to be a friendly activity - not a test.

GETTING TO KNOW PEOPLE - Introductions
Turn to your partner and tell them three things about yourself. Get them to repeat the facts to check if they were listening carefully. Repeat this so that both partners have had a turn. Take your partner and introduce them to another pair.

For example: 'This is Mike. He plays badminton, he enjoys sailing and he has two children called Abigaile and Alex.'

Facilitator: This activity is good for practising listening skills.

USING GAMES

This game will provide an opportunity to talk to the group about what skills we need to teach children to enable them to make friends and maintain friendships. Discuss in pairs and then with the whole group.

Facilitator: When the group have decided on their list of skills show OHP 4 of Friendship Skills (page 62).

RULES

1. Only one person talks at a time. Everyone else listens. The use of the 'magic microphone' or 'talk ticket' will help.

2. Show that you are listening by looking at the person who is speaking.

3. Everyone is included and has a turn.

4. Everyone has the right to have fun. No one can spoil anyone else's fun.

ACTIVE LISTENING

An important aspect of any Circle-time is the skill of 'active listening'. This is a skill that both children and adults need to work at to develop. Active listening means:

1. Focusing on the speaker's needs.

2. Being there for the other person.

3. Showing you understand.

4. Letting the speaker express their feelings without interruptions or 'put-downs'.

5. Common acceptance - that no matter what is said the speaker is still OK.

THE ROUND

'A good friend is someone who…'

THE ACTIVITY

People Bingo

Facilitator: Give out 'bingo cards' (page 55). Ask people to go round and find someone in the group to fit each category. When they find someone they ask them to sign the correct section of the card. Every signature obtained must be different thus ensuring that people circulate and mix. Encourage the participants to ask questions that will give more information about people's interests and hobbies.

Sharing such information is one of the social skills that children need to be taught to enable them to make friends.

I am a vegetarian	I have been to Asia	I can play chess	I can speak a foreign language
I have an interesting hobby	I play squash	I have learnt something new recently	I can play a musical instrument
I wear glasses	I have a pet	I like eating out	I like classical music

 # CONFERENCE

❏ Did anyone find out anything about someone that they didn't know before?

❏ What did they find they had in common with someone else?

❏ Were any of the sections difficult to fill?

❏ Was it easy to share information?

❏ What sort of problems might children have if they completed a similar activity?

 # SPECIAL PERSON

Special Person Car Wash

The group lines up in pairs facing a partner with a small gap in between. The special person for the session stands at the head of the line and walks slowly down between the pairs with their eyes closed. As they pass each group member touches the special person and whispers an affirmation or positive personal message. All this 'washes' over the person and they emerge glowing from the experience!

Facilitator: More than one person can have a go if there is time.

 # GAMES

CONCLUDING GAME - Up

Four people are asked to stand. They can only remain standing for a count of 10. They may sit down before 10 if they wish. As soon as one of the four sits down someone else in the circle must stand up to take their place - again only for a maximum of 10 seconds (people can count in their heads). The object of the game is to make sure there are always four people, and only four people, standing.

Facilitator: This is a fast game and promotes working together co-operatively.

CIRCLE-TIME INSET
Session 5 - Focus on Problem Solving
Time: 3 hours

Facilitator: This session will give ideas and techniques on how problems affecting children and teachers in school can be identified and solutions explored.

 **GAMES**

NAME GAME - Name Juggle

Take a soft ball and throw it to someone in the circle and say their name. The person who catches the ball has to throw it to someone else in the circle and say their name. The game continues until everyone has had a turn. If the group is comprised of individuals who do not know each other then each person says their own name before they throw the ball.

SEATING ARRANGEMENTS

When starting Circle-time we allow the children to sit where they like as this provides a relaxed atmosphere. However, it is possible to move children around by using mixing games which enables the teacher to break up unlikely pairings and encourage a mix of genders. It also allows children to work with different members of the class and talk to children with whom they would not normally make contact.

Mixing games are a fun way to integrate the class:

MIXING GAME - Paint Box

Choose four colours from a paint box and go round the circle giving each person the name of one of the colours. When a colour is called out all the people who have been given that particular one have to get up and find a new seat. When 'Paint Box!' is called out everyone changes place.

USING GAMES

Facilitator: These games should operate smoothly as they are under the direction of the facilitator but it is useful to explain to the group how games can be used as a teaching tool as well as for mixing and affirming people.

RULES

This is also the time to introduce a few simple rules:

1. Only one person talks at a time. Everyone else listens.

2. Show that you are listening by looking at the person who is speaking.

3. Everyone is included and has a turn.

4. Everyone has the right to have fun. No one can spoil anyone else's fun.

It is helpful if rules are written and displayed and referred to when necessary.

ACTIVE LISTENING

Facilitator: An important aspect of any Circle-time activity is the skill of 'active listening'. This is a skill that both children and adults need to work at to develop. Active listening means:

1. Focusing on the speaker's needs.

2. Being there for the other person.

3. Showing you understand.

4. Letting the speaker express their feelings without interruptions or 'put-downs'.

5. Common acceptance - that no matter what is said the speaker is still OK.

ACTIVE LISTENING ACTIVITY
Facilitator: Ask the group to get into the double circles formation where the inner and outer circle face towards each other and each person sits opposite a partner. If the numbers are even then the facilitator observes and if the numbers are odd then the facilitator joins in. Name the pairs A and B.

Facilitator: Tell the group that the A's are to talk and the B's are to listen. Gather the B's out of earshot to give them their instructions.

TASK 1
Person A. Talk to your partner about how you spent your holidays. Talk about the people you like to be with, the places you visited, good meals etc.

Person B. When your partner speaks try to be as *disinterested* as possible. Look around the room, inspect the floor, fiddle with your watch etc. *Do not make eye contact.* Ask a couple of questions, but do not look at your partner. Do not ask for clarification or for more information.

Facilitator: Again gather the B's to give them their instructions in secret.

TASK 2
Person A. Continue to talk about your holiday.

Person B. This time keep interrupting. Try to take over the conversation, talking about your own holiday.

Facilitator: Stop the activity and gather the group.

 **CONFERENCE**

1. Ask the A's - How did you feel talking to someone who was obviously not listening? The feelings could be written up on a 'feelings board'. Did you find it difficult to carry on? What did you do? What did you want to do?

2. Ask the B's - How did you feel - having to ignore what was being said? How much information did you pick up, even though you were trying not to listen?

TASK 3
Person A. Talk to your partner about your dream holiday, with unlimited travel, unlimited expenses, taking anybody of your choice etc.

Person B. This time pay attention! Look at the person, nod, sit slightly forward, *make frequent eye contact*, smile, ask questions, and give further information. Say things like: 'Oh yes! - mm - I see' and give all the information your full, undivided attention. You are now *'active listening'*.

Note to facilitator: Be aware of people becoming uncomfortable during these exercises and stop at the appropriate moment.

CONFERENCE

1. Ask the A's - How did you feel this time? In what way was it different?

2. Ask the B's - How did you feel this time? How much information did you pick up?

Facilitator: Feeling words can again be collected and written on a 'feelings board'.

This is important as it illustrates the need for children to be able to recognise and identify feelings. Extending children's feeling vocabulary is a useful tool for expressing emotions and a starting point to problem solving.

Key points to being a good listener (use OHP 3):

Focus: Give attention/body posture
           Maintain eye contact
           Do not interrupt, offer opinion etc.

Accept: Nod
           Smile
           Show you understand
           Respect

Extend: Ask questions e.g. How did you feel when ...?
           What do you think would happen if ...?
           It seems to me that ...?
           Are you saying that ...?
           Could you say a bit more about ...?
           What do you like most about ...?

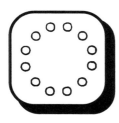

THE ROUND

Facilitator: The group will get another chance to practise their 'active listening' in the next section which is the round. The round is an opportunity for each person to make a statement or contribution to the topic under discussion.

'When I have a problem I ...'

THE ACTIVITY

Group Decisions

Facilitator: This activity illustrates how groups can 'air' problems and come to a consensus on which one to tackle first. Give everyone some coloured sticky dots and a card.

TASK

a) Invite everyone to write a school-based problem or concern on a card and place it on the floor.

b) Find a partner and after discussion, select one concern by placing a coloured dot on the chosen issue.

c) Next get into groups of four, choose one concern and vote by placing a dot on the selected problem. This means people will have to discuss concerns and argue their case for making a choice.

d) Count the dots to find the chosen problem to be discussed.

CONFERENCE

When a single concern has been identified, stay in groups of four and record the following:

Brainstorm
     a) Feelings engendered.
     b) Realistic strategies to help solve this problem.
     c) Select one or two to try.

Feelings	Strategies	Solutions to try

Facilitator: Use the enlarged sheets on page 56.

Also elicit: How well did your group work? What helped/hindered? What have you learnt that may help next time?

SPECIAL PERSON

Facilitator: This is an activity to allow everyone to experience being 'special'. Flower sheets are on page 57.

Affirmation Flowers

1. Organise group into small circles of six.

2. Give everyone an affirmation flower sheet.

3. Ask people to write their name in the leaf.

4. The flowers are passed to the person on the right who has to write a positive comment in one of the petals before passing the sheet to the next person. This continues until all six people have written on all the flowers and the sheet is returned to its owner to be read by them.

Facilitator: This a small memento to take away from the session and keep for those 'rainy day' occasions!

Affirmation Flower

GAMES

CONCLUDING GAME - Non-Verbal Birthday Line-Up

Facilitator: Invite the group to line up in order of their birthdays and to perform the task without talking at all. When all the gesticulations and mimes have finished ask the group to go down the line calling out their date to see if they are all in the correct place. Great fun!

CIRCLE-TIME INSET
Session 6 - Focus on Dealing with Anger
Time: 2 hours

Facilitator: Children who have behaviour problems are often angry, so finding constructive ways of dealing with this emotion can be very beneficial.

 **GAMES**

NAME GAME - Name Echo

One person says the name of someone in the circle and does a simple action or gesture at the same time. The name and action is repeated by the rest of the players one by one round the circle until the named person is reached. They then say the name of someone else further round the circle accompanied by a different gesture. This continues until everyone has had a turn or it feels appropriate to stop.

Facilitator: If a game is failing don't be afraid to stop it and start another one. Be aware of the group mood.

 **RULES**

Facilitator: There could be some sensitive issues discussed during this session so now is the time to introduce a few ground rules about how the group will operate. These will need to be negotiated and agreed by everyone. An element of confidentiality will need to be included so that whatever is said in the circle will remain private to the group.

Suggested rules:
1. Listen to one another.

2. Talk one at a time.

3. Respect the ideas and values of others.

4. Anything said in the circle is confidential.

5. Keep agreements that are made with the group.

ACTIVE LISTENING

Facilitator: When people are angry they are often so immersed in their own emotions they fail to listen to what the other person is saying. An important aspect of any Circle-time activity is the skill of 'active listening'. This is a skill that both children and adults need to work at to develop. *Active listening* means:

1. Focusing on the speaker's needs.

2. Being there for the other person.

3. Showing you understand.

4. Letting the speaker express their feelings without interruptions or 'put-downs'.

5. Common acceptance - that no matter what is said the speaker is still OK.

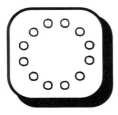

THE ROUND

Facilitator: This is an opportunity to practise 'active listening' as each person is invited to complete the tag line.

'I feel angry when …'

This information could be recorded in the causes of anger section on the 'Dealing With Anger' sheet. (See following page.)

THE ACTIVITY

Facilitator: Ask the group to get into the *double circles* formation where the inner and outer circle face towards each other and each person sits opposite a partner. If the numbers are even then the facilitator observes and if the numbers are odd then the facilitator joins in.

TASK 1

Ask the pairs to discuss what happens when they are angry.

a) How do they feel?

b) What do they do?

Record this information on the 'Dealing with Anger' sheet (page 58).

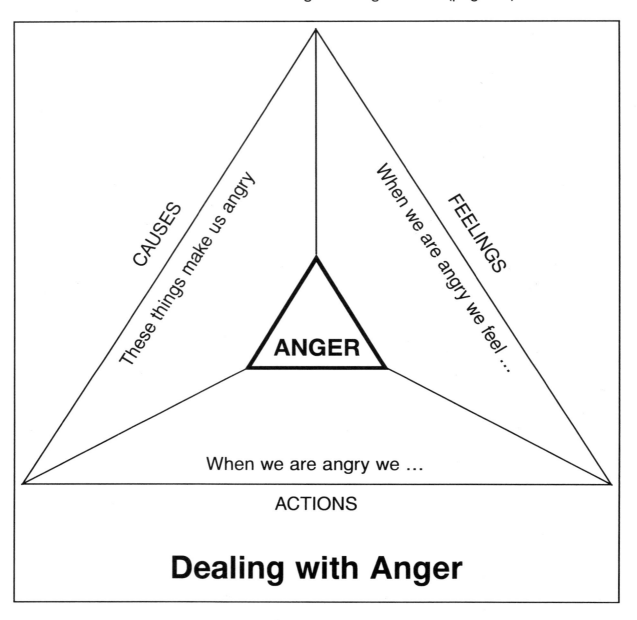

Dealing with Anger

Facilitator: When a large group are in discussion it is useful to have a predetermined signal to gain quiet when you feel they have exhausted the discussion. Shouting above the noise causes tension and is not a good role model. Examples of signals:

❏ An arm raised. When the facilitator raises his or her arm it is a signal for the participants to finish talking and indicate this by also raising their arms.

❏ The word *QUIET PLEASE* written on a piece of card. Hold it up at an appropriate moment and when the whole group has complied then turn the card round to show the other side on which is written *THANK YOU.*

TASK 2
Facilitator: Ask pairs to get into groups of four.

Discuss: a) What are the warning signs?
         b) What helps you to calm down?
           How do you deal with anger?
         c) What would you like other people to do to help you when you
           are feeling angry?

Select a scribe and record the information. For example:

Warning signs	I can calm down by ...	Other people can help by ...
a frown a scowl clenched fists going red in the face out of breath	counting to 10 slowly taking deep breaths talking to someone taking vigorous exercise relaxation techniques	listening to me seeing the funny side leaving me alone for a few minutes giving a different point of view

Facilitator: These sheets will need to be enlarged.

 **CONFERENCE**

Facilitator: Re-form the large circle.

Share the recorded information and look for commonalities and ways of joining or grouping the items together e.g.
    'Many of us feel like hurting others when we are angry.'
or   'Some people really need some space in order to calm down.'
or   'It seems important to most of us that we are listened to or that someone
    cares how we feel.'

How can we express our anger without causing difficulties for others?
Record the ideas and suggestions at an adult level but explain that children can also benefit from shared experiences and solutions which can be collated and displayed in the classroom for reference. A follow-up Circle-time could evaluate solutions that have been tried to ascertain which have been successful.

Building banks of strategies gives children a choice of behaviours.

 **GAMES**

CONCLUDING GAMES

Facilitator: It is important to end this kind of session with something to lighten the tone.

FUN GAME - Hand Game

Everyone is invited to kneel on the floor in the circle, placing their hands flat on the ground. One person taps their left hand once on the floor followed by their right hand. The next person continues in the same way, left, right and so on all round the circle in sequence.

A variation on this is if one person taps the floor twice, the 'action' goes in the reverse direction.

Facilitator: When children play this game they are often tempted to keep repeating the extra action thereby excluding at least half the circle!

In order to make the game fair, make an agreed rule such as, you're only allowed one double tap.

MIXING GAME - Stations

One person stands in the centre of the circle.

Give each person a card with the name of a station. (You could use local place names instead.) The person in the centre calls out two stations who attempt to change places whilst the middle person tries to get one of their seats. If he or she is successful they take the station card. This continues with the option of calling 'All change' if you can't manage to get a seat.

CO-OPERATIVE GAME - Huggy Bears

Players stand in the middle of the circle. Move the chairs back if there is not enough room. Play some lively music to jig about to. When the music is stopped the facilitator calls a number and the players get into groups of that number and give each other a hug. This continues until the group mood tells you it is time to stop. End by calling a number to include all participants and finish with a collective group hug.

CONCLUSION

The activities and ideas in this manual will provide teachers with the basic knowledge and understanding of the Circle-time concept. The six experiential sessions are designed for adult participation but will offer a structure for future planning with their class.

Note to Facilitator: If handouts are required each complete session can be photocopied with the notes to facilitator edited out.

This manual is designed to complement our first book *Personal and Social Education Through Circle-Time* which provides a more detailed explanation of Circle-time and comprehensive lesson plans for use with primary aged children. Initially teachers will need to refer to this when planning sessions for their class. When they have become skilled practitioners they can organise Circle-times to focus on specific areas and needs of their class and children can be encouraged to organise their own sessions. Keeping a record of each Circle-time and evaluating them over a period will help to define strengths and growth points.

All children need to feel happy and secure in order to maximise their learning potential. This will be dependent on positive relationships with the class teacher and their peers. When children feel cared for and valued they will be more able to respond to challenges, both in class and out, and learn coping strategies to manage difficult situations. Positive relationships are enhanced through regular use of Circle-time.

This book is designed for use with teachers - to teach new skills, widen repertoires and increase their understanding of Circle-time. It will provide them with a valuable tool to use and share with their children.

Good luck and happy circling!

Don't confine its use to the classroom. Sit in a circle for staff meetings and make sure everyone is listened to and opinions valued.

Section 3 - Materials

This section contains activity sheets for use with various sessions. Each sheet may be photocopied and given to participants. This section also contains OHP materials and useful reading.

CONTENTS:

Activity Sheet 1 - People Bingo

Activity Sheet 2 - Recording Sheet

Activity Sheet 3 - Affirmation Flower

Activity Sheet 4 - Dealing with Anger

OHP 1 - Circle-time Bullet Points

OHP 2 - Circle-time Structure

OHP 3 - Active Listening

OHP 4 - Friendship Skills

Useful Reading

Activity Sheet 1 - People Bingo

I am a vegetarian	I have been to Asia	I can play chess	I can speak a foreign language
I have an interesting hobby	I play squash	I have learnt something new recently	I can play a musical instrument
I wear glasses	I have a pet	I like eating out	I like classical music

Mollie Curry and Carolyn Bromfield 1997

Activity Sheet 2

FEELINGS	STRATEGIES	SOLUTIONS

Mollie Curry and Carolyn Bromfield 1997

Activity Sheet 3

Name:

Affirmation Flower

Mollie Curry and Carolyn Bromfield 1997

Activity Sheet 4

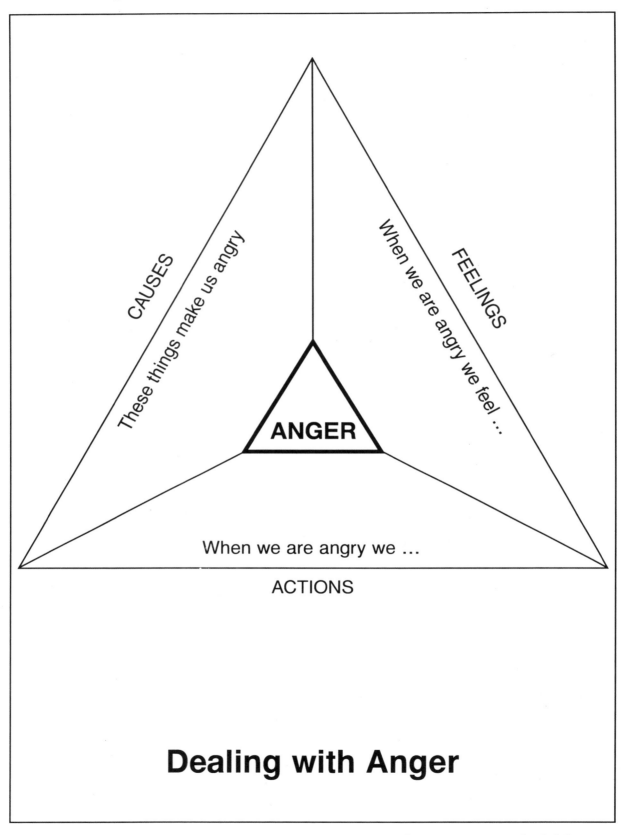

CAUSES
These things make us angry

FEELINGS
When we are angry we feel …

ANGER

When we are angry we …

ACTIONS

Dealing with Anger

Mollie Curry and Carolyn Bromfield 1997

CIRCLE-TIME ...

❏ Develops the unique potential of individuals

❏ Enhances self-esteem

❏ Affirms positive attributes

❏ Builds trust and confidence

❏ Demonstrates how to build & maintain friendships

❏ Explores personal issues

❏ Teaches social skills

❏ Fosters a caring group feeling

❏ Encourages co-operation in the classroom

❏ Examines strategies & solutions for resolving conflicts

❏ Covers the speaking & listening NC targets

❏ Provides a useful tool for shaping desired behaviour

Mollie Curry and Carolyn Bromfield 1997

CIRCLE-TIME STRUCTURE

❏ ## Warm-up Game
Energy raiser
Co-operation and playing together
Using games as a teaching tool

❏ ## A Round
Active listening
Teaching children to be good listeners

❏ ## The Activity
The core section of any Circle-time
The PSE teaching element

❏ ## The Conference
An opportunity to reflect
Extract learning

❏ ## Special Person
Affirming the positive in individuals

❏ ## Concluding Game
Reunite the group

KEY POINTS TO BEING A GOOD LISTENER

FOCUS: Give attention

Lean forward

Maintain eye-contact

Do not interrupt or offer opinions

ACCEPT: Nod and smile

Show you understand

Give respect

EXTEND: Ask questions such as:

Are you saying that …?

How did you feel when …?

It seems to me that …?

Could you say a bit more about …?

What do you think about …?

Mollie Curry and Carolyn Bromfield 1997

FRIENDSHIP SKILLS

- ❏ Saying hello/goodbye

- ❏ Beginning/ending a conversation

- ❏ How to join in an activity or game

- ❏ Playing a game

- ❏ Winning and losing

- ❏ Suggesting an activity or game

- ❏ Asking someone for help

- ❏ Offering help to someone

- ❏ Giving a compliment

- ❏ Accepting a compliment

- ❏ Expressing your feelings

- ❏ Showing understanding of another's feelings

- ❏ Asking permission

- ❏ Apologising

- ❏ Negotiating

- ❏ Sharing/taking turns

- ❏ Body language/eye-contact/personal space

Mollie Curry and Carolyn Bromfield 1997

USEFUL READING

CIRCLE-TIME

Bliss, T. and Robinson, G. (1995) *Developing Circle-time*. Lucky Duck Publishing: Bristol.

Bromfield, C. (1992) *The Effectiveness of Circle-time as a Strategy for Use in the Primary School with Special Regard to Children Having Behaviour Problems.* Unpublished M.Ed (SEN) Dissertation. University of Plymouth.

Curry, M. and Bromfield, C. (1994) *Personal and Social Education for Primary Schools Through Circle-time.* NASEN Enterprises Ltd: Tamworth.

Mosley, J. (1993) *Turn Your School Round*. LDA: Cambridge.

Mosley, J. (1996) *Quality Circles*. LDA: Cambridge.

FEELINGS

Amos, J. (1990) *Feelings: Lonely.* Cherrytree Press Ltd.

Curry, M. (1997) 'Providing Emotional Support through Circle-time'. *Support for Learning.* Vol. 12, No. 3.

Hall, E. et al. (1990) *Scripted Fantasy in the Classroom*. Routledge: London.

Masheder, M. (1986) *Let's Co-operate*. Peace Education Project.

Morris, L. & Perkins, G. (1991) *Remembering Mum.* A. & C. Black: London.

Plant, S. & Stoate, P. *Loss and Change.* PEP.

Wood, A. & Richardson, R. (1992) *Inside Stories.* Trentham Books.

SELF-ESTEEM

Anderson, J. *Thinking, Changing, Re-arranging.* Metamorphous Press.

Borba, M. & Borba, D. (1978) (1982) *Self-Esteem* (Volumes 1 & 2). Harper & Row: London.

Burns, R. B. (1979) *The Self-Concept.* Longman: London.

Canfield, J. & Wells, H. C. (1976) *100 Ways to Enhance Self-Esteem in the Classroom.* Prentice Hall: London.

Coopersmith, S. (1981) *The Antecedents of Self-Esteem.* Freeman Press.

Illsley-Clarke, J. (1978) *Self-Esteem - A Family Affair.* Harper & Row: London.

Lawrence, D. (1987) *Enhancing Self-Esteem in the Classroom.* PCP Education Ltd.

Purkey, W. W. (1970) *Self-Concept and School Achievement.* Prentice Hall.

White, M. (1991) *Self-Esteem.* Daniels Publishing.

FRIENDSHIP

Fountain, S. (1990) *Learning Together.* W.W.F. and Stanley Thornes: Cheltenham.

Masheder, M. (1989) *Let's Play Together.* Green Print, The Merlin Press.

Masheder, M. (1991) *Let's Co-operate.* Peace Pledge Union: London.

Rawlins, G. & Rich, J. *Look, Listen and Trust.* Nelson.

Roffey, S. (1994) *Young Friends.*

Ross, C. & Ryan, A. (1991) *Can I Stay in Today, Miss? Improving the School Playground.* Trentham Books: Stoke-on-Trent.

Thorne, B. (1993) *Gender Play: Girls and Boys in School.* OUP: Oxford.

PROBLEM SOLVING

Blatchford, P. (1989) *Playtime in the Primary School.* NFER-Nelson.

Drew, N. (1987) *Learning the Skills of Peacemaking.* Jalmar Press.

Galloway, F. (1989) *Personal and Social Education in the Primary School.* Pergamon Press.

Holland, S. & Ward, C. (1990) *Assertiveness: A Practical Approach.* Winslow Press.

Kingston Friends Workshop Group (1985) The Handbook of Kingston Friends Workshop Group, *Ways and Means: An Approach to Problem Solving.*

DEALING WITH ANGER

Brown, C., Barnfield, J. & Stone, M. (1990) *Spanner in the Works.* Trentham Books: Stoke-on-Trent.

Fugitt, E. (1973) *He Hit Me Back First.* Jalmar Press.

Grunsell, A. (1989) *Let's Talk about Bullying.* Gloucester Press.

Judson, S. (1984) *A Manual on Non Violence and Children.* New Society Publishers.

Kreidler, W. J. (1984) *Creative Conflict Resolution.* Scott, Foresman & Co.

Miller, B. & T. (1990) *That's Not Fair!* RMEP PRESS.

Nicholas, F. M. (1987) *Coping with Conflict.* LDA: Cambridge.

Sanders, P. (1994) *Feeling Violent.* Gloucester Press.